How to Discover the Entrepreneur in You

SIGNS YOU MIGHT BE AN ENTREPRENEUR

An eye-opening guide that
emphasizes the value of
entrepreneurship in the business
world today

SHARIFAH HARDIE

Edition 2019

The trademarks that are used are without any consent and the publication of the trademark is without permission or backing by the trademark owner. All trademarks and brands within this book are for clarifying purposes and are the owned by the owners themselves, not affiliated to with this document.

DISCLAIMER

The contents of this book have been checked and compiled with great care. For the completeness, correctness and topicality of the contents however no guarantee or guarantee can be taken over. The content of this book represents the personal experience and opinion of the author and is for entertainment purposes only. There will be no legal responsibility or liability for damages resulting from counterproductive exercise or errors by the reader. No guarantee can be given for success. The author therefore assumes no responsibility for the non-achievement of the goals described in the book.

Table of Contents

AUTHOR'S BIO

Sharifah Hardie, also known as Ask Sharifah, is CEO of XRoadsTV.com, InTheNewsPR.com and InTheNewsMagazine.com.

Ms. Hardie is a business consultant, online marketing specialist, and influencer. With over twenty five years of business experience, Sharifah Hardie has positioned herself to be one of the top executives in entertainment and a person on the rise.

Ms. Hardie served a key role as a Consultant and as Director of Marketing of Punch TV Studios. As such, she was able to assist the company to expand its reach, gain national exposure and raise millions of dollars in its Initial Public Offering (IPO).

Ms. Hardie has been able to harness the power of the Internet to build successful businesses, while simultaneously reducing costs since the 90s. Her innovative style brings fresh ideas to the ever-changing landscape of business, technology, entertainment, media, marketing and advertising.

Ms. Hardie firmly guides brands in such a way that they speak to audiences. She is an expert at being able to take calculated risks to design new levels of recognition and acceptance for the businesses she works with.

Along with being an incredibly intuitive Expert and Influencer, Sharifah Hardie is also a published author. Her first book, "And Here's Your Box – From Laid Off to Loving Life" shared how she became Google's #1 Ranked, "Professional Business Consultant" by overcoming disappointments, life lessons and victories with a bottom-line technique that reaps success for devoted listeners.

Visit Sharifah at AskSharifah.com

1

ENTREPRENEURSHIP. BORN OR LEARNED?

Have you noticed the whole world seems to be headed in the direction of change and innovation? You probably already knew that but the strangest part is that most people think that they are entrepreneurs. The new trend going around is that everyone can start a business and should start a business if they want to succeed in life. I completely disagree with this research. It's true that owning a business can mean a break from a job that you mandatory go to every day but it may also spell doom to those who go there for the wrong reasons.

To fully discuss it, we must have a clear and defined meaning of an entrepreneur. The dictionary definition of an entrepreneur is, "one who organizes, manages, and assumes the risks of a business or enterprise". The word 'entrepreneur' comes from the word *enterprise* which means the ability or desire to do dangerous or difficult things or solve problems in new ways. An entrepreneur must be one willing to solve problems in new ways, must be able to look at the future and see something different. They should be able to take on the risk with or without fear of losing or winning.

Just because someone starts a business, doesn't automatically make him/her an entrepreneur. But I won't be taking sides with whether entrepreneurs are born or if it is a learned skill. Every child has dreams, every person wants to become something. Just ask a normal four-year-old what they wish to be in future and you hear a lot of cool stuff. With the span of time, you eventually see the end of what they became. It's either they made their dreams come true or they didn't, no fence. My reference to this is that entrepreneurs are not just ordinary business owners or startups; they are business owners with clearly defined dreams, vision and a passion that drives them to ensure that their goals are met.

A good example will be a laundry business. Here are two individuals, probably even friends that decide they want to start up a business. We'll call the first Andrew and the second Peter. So Andrew has very different motives from starting his business, he wants to make profit, huge profits and that's all. But here's Peter, he wants to change the way you think about laundry service and probably the way clothes are packaged. Andrew and Peter both had jobs at a particular laundry company but they decided to leave and start up their own companies. Andrew doesn't want to be bossed around, he clearly loves the laundry work but he wants to be his own boss. He is tired of working 8- 5 every day and imagines having his own business where he could check in when he wishes and make lots of revenue doing so.

Peter too, wants to be his own boss. He discovered there was a problem with the way his previous job handled the laundry and knows that the only way he could provide the best service is to create his own company. So the two friends start out, little cash in hand but with great determination. Jumping to the end of the story, Andrew is out of business, and wonders why he hates the laundry work while Peter is relaxing in a well-furnished home, with over 50 different branches of his laundry company at various locations of the country.

What happened to both of them along the way? They had the same experience at their previous place, wanted to create revenue and also started their own business. Let's find out what made them different.

2

SO YOU THINK YOU'RE AN ENTREPRENEUR- WHAT YOU DON'T KNOW?

In the previous chapter, you might think I am a little biased in the story but that scenario plays out every working day. The whole entrepreneur thing again; what then really is the difference?

FACT 1- Entrepreneurs are dreamers

Surprised? I hoped not. Look at the biggest companies today, Coca-Cola, Apple, Microsoft, IBM, McDonald's, Ford and just name it. They have a common similarity about them. Their founders were all dreamers. When I use the word *dream*, I don't mean they slept on their beds dreaming their lives away, I certainly hope that's not what you think. They had a VISION. That is what makes two stores selling exactly the same thing but when you go to one, there is something that just clicks about them. It could be the way they treat their customers, or that they pay attention to details or something. If you're thinking that the competition will reduce to make room for you or these big companies had a better chance in the past than now, then you're dead wrong. In their starting points, people were as resistant to change as they are now, but they saw something most of their competition didn't and that made them different.

FACT 2- Entrepreneurs experience FAILURES a lot

This is a sure-banker for anyone that thinks he/she is an entrepreneur. You are going to fail probably even more times than you planned for. Entrepreneurship is a risk on its own. The coin has two sides and for first timers, the tails are more likely to show up till you can flip your coin well. Every and any entrepreneur didn't make it at first. They all failed. So if you started a business and it seems everything is failing, great news, you are on the right path. But just because you failed at first doesn't mean you won't succeed at the end. Failure is a part of life and a greater part of the risk involved in being an entrepreneur. So if you are scared of failure, you could deal with it and accept it now or you could chicken out and remain bound for the rest of your life (a little tough love to start the day).

FACT 3 – Entrepreneurs aren't always the best in their fields

You always see that one very talented guy in the office that ran off to start his business and in a few years' time, he looks worse than you possibly imagine. Entrepreneurs most often than not are not even close to the best people in their field. You can easily classify them as average but this doesn't mean that really smart people can't be entrepreneurs, but it is rare to find. Entrepreneurs may not even know the in and out of the business as well as some others but as I said earlier, they have a Vision. They see the future and are ready to risk their whole lives to make it happen.

3

THE ENTREPRENEUR, THE TECHNICIAN, AND THE MANAGER

Building a successful business means you have to be more than just an entrepreneur. You have to be three persons in one. Though at different stages, you drop some quality of one and pick up more of the other, that is the evidence of a growing entrepreneur with his business. Always remember that your business will always reflect who you are and how you do things. If you're careless and pay little attention to details, it will show in the way you do business. This is the more reason the entrepreneur has to keep investing and improving himself to ensure his business does the same.

Back to our illustration in the previous chapter of Andrew and Peter. Let's discover how they handled their own three unique personalities that make up for what we call their entrepreneurial ability.

- **The entrepreneur.** The entrepreneur is the dreamer, the imaginer, the one with the sparks in the eyes and looks at every problem as an opportunity to be a turning point. The entrepreneur doesn't exist in today's world. He lives in the future, in tomorrow, the place of possibilities and the world of the impossible. This is the more reason why most successful entrepreneurs aren't surprised when the future plays out the way they've seen it. They lived them already and as soon as it becomes today, they move into tomorrow. They don't give up, they are passionate about change. The entrepreneur is happy when he is allowed to design new worlds; they are called innovators in business. So the entrepreneur sees the world today different from the average person. Since he lives in the future, he wants the present to reflect that and since most people can't seem to view it like him, he sometimes creates more havoc in a bid to control people to get to his scene. To the entrepreneur, the world is full of opportunities but the people are the problem, they are too slow. Peter in our story is an entrepreneur. He sees the opportunity that nobody sees despite the problems. Andrew, on the other hand, sees the opportunity to just be free from his boss.

- **The manager.** The manager is logical. Without the manager, things would go out of order. The unpredictable entrepreneur needs the manager to put things in place. The manager lives in the past. He craves order while the former craves control. The manager strives on consistency, cares little for change. Where the entrepreneur sees opportunity, the manager sees problems. The manager isn't as change motivated as the entrepreneur. He loves to do things the way they have always been done. 'Things must be in order, we don't do that here', 'that's great but not now', 'according to the company's policies…', these are all examples of the way the manager reacts. But we don't hate the manager; no. The manager puts things in its place. The entrepreneur creates, the manager arranges and cleans up the mess of the entrepreneur. What a harmony. The whole business mindset is the manager while the entrepreneur is the innovator.

- **The technician.** The technician lives in the present (you guessed correctly). He loves work. 'Love' is a big understatement, he lives to work. The technician loves to do. Things aren't just meant to be dreamed of, they should be acted upon. He adores the process of working and ensuring that things get moving. He is at his peak when he's working, and works steadily in a flow, his mind ever focused on the work. The technician has little time to think. Thinking is a waste of productive hours and obstructs the flow. He isn't interested in ideas but on how to do it. Without the technician, there would be dreamers and perfectionist; no real work will be accomplished. Everyone hinders him, the entrepreneur is a problem as he keeps creating more work for him than he has experience for or knows how to handle. The manager tries to fit him into what you can call a 'closet', just to complete the puzzle and put things in place. The technician hates being treated this way, work is what he does and not just a system of results.

The manager becomes a problem to the technician as a meddler in his daily affairs and the manager sees the technician as a problem, a round peg in a square hole in need of management. The entrepreneur is the one who caused the whole trouble in the beginning. So how do they all cooperate to give the best result? We all have these three personalities fighting to gain control of our beings. But still there lies a balance in them. The entrepreneur could keep dreaming, the manager could create the working environment and the technician could keep doing the work he loves. But we hardly see this balance in real life. Most business owners are probably 10% entrepreneur, 40% managers, and 50% technicians. The entrepreneur wakes up with a vision, the manager frets out and the technician goes out to start a business, as he struggles to break free of the two. Andrew here is a technician, he loves to work. He wants to be free from his bosses and now he is free. He doesn't stop to think of why this business. No, thinking is for losers, he is a doer. But Peter is a dreamer; he wants to effect change and not just work. They start up their companies. Here's what happens.

4

THE THREE STAGES
OF A BUSINESS

Every business goes through three stages. Infancy, adolescent, and maturity. Though a business can start out from maturity, they would still need to pass through the stages again. The different stage is because businesses grow just like people. But if the people within the business refuse to grow, then the business starts dying.

This happens when a technician runs the business. Andrew was the best at his previous job. He knew the work so well and can do it better than most of them so he starts his own company.

THE INFANCY STAGE

The technician is free from his old boss and can do his thing. Nothing is too much that he can't do. He devotes long hours every day into working optimistically. He only cares about the work he does, so he keeps going at it. He is in for a surprise, he now has to do the work he knows how to do and the work he doesn't know how. He doesn't just have to do laundry; he is responsible for customers, for the bookkeeping, for the accounting, for delivery, for everything. He has to do it all, whether he likes it or not.

No one is going to help anyway. It is his business. In infancy, the business is not separate from the owner; they are one and the same. He works hard and hard work pays. He gets customers, they keep coming back. A professional hand did their laundry. He's really good at it. Suddenly something happens. He loses his touch. He bleached the wrong clothes, he didn't deliver on time, there's nobody to answer the customers at the front desk, complaints start coming. Something has gone seriously wrong and you can tell. All of a sudden, he wished he didn't have to come work anymore, he wants to hide, the work seems to have no ending, the cycle keeps going on and there is no break. He has to come to work every day and do everything himself. What used to seem fine no longer is. The business is now the new boss and this time there is no getting rid of it. Then Andrew either evolves or shuts down the business. Infancy stage ends the moment the owner realizes that just doing the work by himself isn't enough. He needs help.

ADOLESCENT STAGE

When he gets help to handle what he can't present at the moment, then adolescent stage has begun. The business has grown and can't just accommodate him alone. So he puts up a job vacancy sign and specifies what he wants help for. He needs someone to take customer's calls, to keep accounts and to deliver. He requires a person with experience. He needs someone to do the work he doesn't like to do.

The very first employee is hired - let's call her Mabel. Mabel knows the work well and shows efficiency in handling it. She can answer the calls and keep the accounts while attending to customers. Andrew is happy; he can focus on work, sweet work. He doesn't have to worry about those kinds of things again; Mabel is handling them just fine. Mabel sees one clear thing as she has always done in all her years of experience; he has no idea what he's doing. But she stays all along. It's her job, she fixes things.

He doesn't have to worry about her work again. She can do it all, that's what she was hired for. The manager in him awakes but he never knew there was a manager so he hands her all the work. Mabel only comes to him when she needs help and she does her job pretty much better than he could ever have done. But Mabel needs more help, she needs someone to make deliveries, to pick up the calls and welcome clients while she focuses on the account. Andrew allows her to hire more people. She does and then the problems begin again.

He sees the way the clothes are packaged, that's not how this is done. Haven't you being properly orientated? Andrew wonders and does it. Things start happening, customers complain of the service they received. There was a problem with clothing, he handles it himself. Work was supposed to be easier. What has gone wrong? The employees are sloppy; nobody works as hard as him or is willing to? He can do much better than the service they give now. Andrew decides to do the work by himself. He won't leave his company to just anyone. The manager in him isn't trained yet so he takes it all back. He fires the workers and starts small again. Then the cycle happens, nobody is satisfied, not him, not the customer and definitely not the service. The business dies gradually till he eventually shuts down or Andrew learn and tried better.

THE MATURITY STAGE

Maturity is the final stage of every business. It is not a status acquired and kept at a constant level, but a stage that implies it can advance and grow without much threat to its existence. A mature business has clearly defined who they are, what they stand for and what they do. They are completely aware of how and why it works there. The importance of having a vision before starting up a company is to enable you to start at the mature stage. Most big-time businesses started here. They knew exactly what they wanted to achieve.

In the illustration, Peter is the entrepreneur and he knows clearly what he wants to achieve by going into the business. He is not motivated by freedom from his previous bosses but by a chance to create a difference in the industry. He sees the future then comes back to the present to see how to create that future. That is what a mature business is. Andrew's business will have a lower lifespan because he doesn't have a place for the business. A journey with no destination will always lead to nowhere.

The maturity stage is where the model of the business is birthed. It is the 'how we do it here' definition. Any business owner that cannot define their destination or how they see themselves in the next years is headed for failure on a one-way ticket. This is the major difference between Andrew and Peter. The success factor is quite small in comparison to the losses if it is absent.

5

MYTHS ABOUT ENTREPRENEURSHIP

1. Risk Takers

Entrepreneurs definitely take a lot of risks but the myth here is they go out and gamble it all away. There is something called a calculated risk. Entrepreneurs do not just take risks blindly and hope luck will help them, rather they check out the opportunities and if they have a strong belief that it will turn out well, they go for it. Still, there are some opportunities they just walk in on and they throw all of themselves in. However, they still check their risk margin and know for certain that their chances of winning are greater. This is also one reason for failures in entrepreneurship.

2. Entrepreneurs are born.

This will be inconclusive as earlier because whether you are born talented or without, there is no law that limits you from going after your dreams but you. The only box is in our mind, the only limit is the boundary we place on our abilities. I have seen entrepreneurs that change things even though they were ordinary and without any special ability. It takes one to dream and believe in it long enough, then to achieve it.

3. Entrepreneurs are driven by money.

The money factor is one area that most people love to see good businesses. They have money yes, but look closely and look closer still. Majority of successful businesses started not because they were driven by money. They wanted change. As the saying goes, necessity is the mother of innovation; it becomes more evident that you would want change because you are tired of the status quo. You want to create the world you envision. Money is just a means to an end and not the end in itself. It is the tool that gives you the leverage to create the masterpiece and not the masterpiece itself.

4. *Entrepreneurs have no personal life, they are workaholics.*

This is certainly a myth. Being an entrepreneur at first may mean you give many hours to your business but it shouldn't deprive you of your life away from work. It should rather give you more time if you built it well. There is a certain company in Japan that doesn't allow their workers to work overtime no matter the situation of urgency. They respect your personal time and encourage you to live and work not live to work. This is an example of true entrepreneurship; it allows you to breathe while working.

5. *You need the experience to start a business.*

There is something I love very much and it's called learning on the job. To start a business you need to know some few things but you don't need so much experience as they claim. Research shows that the less experience you have, the higher your chances of succeeding. Experience is vital but it will be more fun and yet painful learning from everyday mistakes and taking on new risks rather than trying to avoid the loopholes you learned from.

6. *Entrepreneurs are ruthless and cunning.*

This is a popular belief. People see entrepreneurs as though they would do anything possible to get their way. I do not disagree with that but I don't agree fully. Any successful entrepreneur knows that success doesn't just lie in their dreams but also in their ability to work well with others. They don't have to step over people to prove points. Being ruthless will cause your business everything; the name, the brand and the dream. The myth that being an entrepreneur will make you ruthless is wrong except in cases when winning becomes a do or die affair and creates unhealthy competition among people. The entrepreneur will lose his best people, his team, his customers and eventually lose it all if he is ruthless or cunning.

7. *The only prerequisite is to have a great idea.*

I have been pushing the idea of having an idea quite hard but the truth still remains. You need the manager and the technician in order to actually succeed in business. Just thinking about it isn't enough, you have to take action. Entrepreneurs are people of action, not just ideas. Don't be misled that entrepreneurship is just about ideas or invention of something new. It isn't just that. It is how you can sell a similar product in a different way or solve overlooked problems.

6

WHY A
CORPORATION?

First of all, let's define what a corporation is. A corporation is a business that is separate from the owner legally and the business stands alone as an entity. This means that you are not seen as your business no matter your stake-holding. Most small businesses are sole proprietorship so they are recognized as the same as their owners but the big guns know better.

If you truly want a big company and a brand that lasts, incorporation is king. You should build a business that outlives you and can live without you. Making your business its own person will not only open doors for better investment and funding opportunities but also better planning.

Incorporating your business is necessary for a lot of reasons and some are:

1. **Your personal assets are secured.**

Corporations give you the advantage of building your wealth away from the business. You don't have to be sued to court for mismanagement or some other reasons at all. You are not responsible for the losses and your private property will not be sold to pay back loans incurred by the business. Sounds great right! As an entrepreneur, you would also want something more than just the regular income you received from the business and you can indeed be richer than your business. A proper business should have a structure that protects the liabilities of its owners

2. **Your business credibility status increases.**

This is very true. Your business will be seen as a person of its own where other people can invest. It opens it up for expansion possibilities and for better opportunities. Most of the largest businesses today are not run by one person as a sole proprietor but as large corporations. They have more finances and can get things done easily.

3. **The brand of the business is protected.**

Making your business a corporation will protect the reputation of the business. Your reputation will have very little effect on the company's profile. People see the business and what it does differently from you.

You are free to give expression to yourself away from the business.

4.   Continuous existence.

Corporations exist even when their founders are dead or away from the business. This is one key advantage of owning a corporation. The business can outlive the owner.

5.   Tax benefits.

Many corporations enjoy tax benefits that are not available for privately owned small businesses. Corporations also have access to loan facilities and investment opportunities.

7

FAMOUS ENTREPRENEURS TO LEARN FROM

In entrepreneurship, always strive to copy from the best. Take their advice, see their steps. Anything genuine is always able to replicate. There are so many successful entrepreneurs today in which you can learn from. I have chosen a few examples and advice they have.

1. Tony Robbins. Tony is an entrepreneur, best-selling author, and philanthropist. He is a recognized authority on leadership and psychology. He had served as an advisor to world leaders and he is the author of five international best selling books. His advice to entrepreneurs is, 'the most painful mistake I see in first-time entrepreneurs is thinking that just having a business plan or a great concept is enough to guarantee success. It's not. Business success is 80% psychology and 20% mechanics...The biggest thing that will hold you back is your own nature...'

2.   Guy Kawasaki. Guy is the evangelist for Canva and author of thirteen books which have been hailed as a great weapon for entrepreneurs. He was the former chief evangelist for Apple. His business advice 'my business tip is to focus on the prototype. Don't focus on your pitch deck, business plan or financial projections. If you get your prototype out, and you get enough people using it, you never have to write a business plan......'

3.   Steve Jobs. Steve is the founder of Apple and an entrepreneurial legend. He famously started Apple in a garage with co-founder Steve Wozniak in 1976 after dropping out of college. The company has a market capitalization of $870 billion. According to Jobs, two things are required to build a successful company: passion and people.

4.   Bill Gates. Gates is the co-founder of Microsoft with Paul Allen. He became the world's youngest billionaire at the age of 31. Gates believed that change should be continuous and consistent. It's no wonder Windows updates itself frequently. According to Bill Gates, to become successful, it important to take the risk. And to ensure success, you have to strategize and plan well.

5.   Elon Musk. Musk is an innovative entrepreneur. He's built and launched innovative rocket ships and landed one. He laid the groundwork for online payments through his work at PayPal. He is helping to save the environment with electric Tesla and is even laying the foundation for the first human trip to Mars. He advises that money shouldn't be your main goal, fail forward with a plan and embrace your worst case scenario.

8

FRANCHISING – THE SECRET TO LONG LASTING BUSINESSES

Taking a great deal of research from the largest companies, you can truly notice a trend. They are all doing something very similar that worked for them. Take a look at McDonald's. This business is one of the fastest growing businesses, serving food to more than 42 million people every day in about 120 countries. How did they do it? By franchising. Ray Kroc created a business model upon which an entire generation of successful entrepreneurs have built their fortunes. Coca-Cola is one of the companies that have used this method to continue remaining in business for as long as it possibly can.

Business franchising format has reported a success rate of new independently owned business. Where 80% of all businesses fail in the first five years, 75 % of franchises succeed. The reason for this success is the creation of a business model otherwise called a prototype. The model is a place where all assumptions are put into test in the real world. The question to be asked is 'Does it work?' If it does, then the franchisor aims to show how it works and the system starts from there.

Franchising is mainly about how something works. The system runs the business and the people run the system. The system becomes the solution to the problems that have beset all businesses. The business becomes a machine or a game that can run on its own without any added motivation going at its own objectives. The franchise is a model of a business that works. Recall our illustration, Peter started his company from the maturity stage, he clearly knew how he wanted his business to work and how the process was going to take place.

Franchising is the core of every great business in the world. The question is how to create your own prototype for a system that works. Peter understood that his business was not his life and it was important to separate these two aspects. Your prototype should be able to be replicated over 1000 times and more. It will provide consistent values to everyone in it and the model should be operated with the lowest possible level of skill required. All work operations should be documented in the operations manuals and any amendment will be updated in it.

To build a franchise prototype, there are three things necessary to pursue in its evolution. Innovation, quantification, and orchestration.

Innovation

Innovation is the act of introducing new ideas, devices, and methods. Innovation is not just about creativity or introducing new ideas but also about putting those ideas into the real world. To the franchisor, the process by which the business does business is a marketing tool. Every part of the system is a means to stamp a mark of uniqueness on the mind of the consumers. Innovation is the heart of exceptional businesses. Innovation must always take the customer's point of view. At the same time, innovation simplifies your business to critical essentials. It should make things easier for you and the people of your business. Innovation is known as the best way to produce a high level of energy in every company.

Quantification

Innovation needs to be quantified to be effective. Quantification relates to the impact of innovation. How would you determine how the changes you make in the company reflect on your revenue? How do you measure the effects of new things? This is what quantification is all about. And it is obvious that it must be addressed by quantification at the outset of the business development process. Without numbers, you can't know where you stand and where you're going.

Orchestration

After innovating and identifying the effect of it on your business, then it's time to orchestrate it. Orchestration means doing something consistently until it becomes a part of your operations. The innovations need to be implanted in such a way that it can easily be added to the work processes for the company.

9

BUSINESS DEVELOPMENT PROGRAM- THE PROCESS

To create the prototype of your business, you need a business plan. They are so many self-help books out there that help to write business plans but I have a simplified form that works for you. It's not rocket science, it's actually easy. You can create the best business plan that works for you. Remember that your business will always reflect who you are. The business plan is composed of five distinct steps:

1. Your goal/ambition.

2. Your strategic objective.

3. Your organizational strategy.

4. Your management strategy.

5. Your people strategy.

Your goal/ambition

Recall, your business will reflect your personality so you want to work on yourself first. You need to know your own values, who you want to become and what kind of life you need. You don't need a self-help book to determine what kind of life you want to live. You need to be intentional in creating your own world. The first step in your business is defining what you actually want for yourself. Most major businesses are reflections of their owners. The excellent business reveals an excellent business owner. Without your primary goals, you would just be working for the sake of keeping busy and making money. There would be no achievement, no progress and no measure of how far you have gone. Take time out and write out your life's goals and ambition and how your business will help you create your ideal life.

Your strategic objective

Once you have a picture of the life you want, your strategic objective will be the means to get you started in the direction. The strategic objective is a clear statement of what your business will do, to enable you to achieve your primary goal. Your strategic objective is not a business plan but a list of standards. It is a tool for measuring your progress towards a specific end. It is a template for your business to make certain that the time you invest in it produces exactly want you to want from it.

The first standard is money. How much money will you require to live your ideal life? How much will your business generate for you to classify it as meeting the goal? You may not know exactly now but you should set an aim for it.

The second standard is about the opportunity worth pursuing. What type of business will help you meet your goal? Does the business you wish to do have the ability to give you satisfaction or fulfill your aims. How would your customer feel about your business? Who is your customer? You can't have a niche for everything except you produce everything. What demographic does your business reach?

The third standards are specific questions that need to be answered. When will your prototype be complete? Where will business end, nationally, internationally, locally? How are you going into business, retail or wholesale? What standards will you insist on?

Your organization strategy

It is never too early to organize your business. Most companies organize around people rather than functions. Even if you haven't started out your business, you should state out the process for doing things and the functions and roles of everyone in the business. Write out all the various positions available and state their roles. Even if you're the only one yet, still define it. As your business grows, more roles will come up and you can change it to adapt to changing roles but never leave your business structure-less. Have a process for new employees and new workers. By organizing your business, you can create a system that will work without you. You have to keep consistent at it and keep reminding people of the process to maintain the standard.

Your management strategy

You don't need to find great people with so many experiences in management skills. What you need is a great strategy for work. As a manager, you may not always be around to check on your company but your system of doing things should. The system becomes a strategy. In defining your prototype, no stone should be left unturned. Paying attention to details as to how, for example, the furniture is arranged is as important as how customers are treated. There should be a kind of checklist process for every worker to be able to easily replicate the work. Everyone should be oriented on this as the business grows.

Your people strategy

This strategy is on how to motivate your workers to do anything. How do you get your people to work? It's simple, create a game. Not an actual video game but a business game. Games are quite addictive and have rules that define how they are played. Your system is your game. Ensure that the game is kept running, and doesn't end. The moment it ends, your business dies. The moment you get bored, your business dies. Create a process that will encourage others to work more and play the game without knowing. Create the business game, then get them playing. Play your own game and respect change without changing standards.

Your marketing strategy

There is no business without the customer. Your marketing strategy will depend on your customer demography. Try to visualize your customer. Your customer is continuously making decisions about you even without their notice. You should be able to get the attention of your customer amongst the competition. You should be able to get it in their minds that once they need the product they think first of you. You should study your market and understand what moves it.

10

STARTING SMALL

As important as it is to plan for the business, you can keep planning from now to tomorrow, but if you don't start, nothing will change. Most great businesses you never heard about are still on paper and there are cemeteries full of multi-billion dollar business ideas. The first rule of work is to work. Never plan without the commitment to begin. To fail you must start, to succeed you must also start. But since you're armed with the knowledge to overcome risks on the way, your chances of failure are reduced by 50%.

The starting point matters a lot more than what most people think. It is not enough to have a good plan on paper when you don't take actions. Don't just say it, show it.

Starting small is about starting despite the present situation. There would never be a better time than now. No time is perfect until you choose to make it so. Depending on the business, most startups do not require as much capital as you think. Sometimes it just requires you and your computer. Regardless, if you don't start you would never even have the chance to succeed.

Far more important than that, starting small helps you test-run your business prototype. You've planned it all on paper, then check to see if it works. It gives you the advantages of easily correcting your mistakes at the lowest cost. Most big businesses today lose millions on mistakes that you would never believe possible. Still, that should never stop you from trying out new things. The beginning is more important. In our illustration, Andrew and Peter, despite their end results would never have known what went right or wrong if they hadn't begun.

Some important tips to know when starting up a company are:

1.   Avoid excuses.

There can never be too much emphasis placed on this subject. Don't let excuses, emotions or feelings get in the way of your dreams. Decide; take action before checking your emotions. You will wake up certain mornings and even when you think you are all about your dream the previous day, you might not get that euphoria the next. Stop making excuses why you can't start or why it won't work. Try it. Start it.

2. Don't ignore advice.

You may not follow through on it or it may just sound plain wrong to you but listening to advise from others is an effective way to grow your company. It helps you form opinions not streamlined by certain beliefs. The world is a large and open place, it would do you well to open up and listen to what people are saying. Ideas lay in simple talks not always the big one.

3. Think from the customer to you and back.

Your idea is great but how will the customer view it. How does the market see it? What problems will it achieve? Entrepreneurship is about solving problems. Your company should have a specific problem it wants to solve.

4. Keep it simple.

This statement always goes for almost everything, simple is always sophisticated. In drawing your business plan and prototype, try your possible best to keep it simple. Yes, it's a profession but the simplicity will enable anyone to be able to understand it and truly blend with it. Your work processes should be clear, precise and easy to understand. The theory that if you can't explain it to a seven-year-old, then you don't know it applies here too. Make sure anyone can get in on the plan.

5.   Plan for the bad days.

Though nobody prays this would come but it does anyway so rather than wish it away or totally ignore it, plan for it. Plan your emergency protocol. Plan for what to do if everything comes crashing down; it is never a bad idea to have backups without shutting down the company.

6.   Speak up. Tell others.

Businesses grow with referrals, reviews, and information. Don't just keep quiet about it. Let others know what you do. Someone might be in need of a service you can render or might just link you up with your biggest clients. There is always value in human relationships and interaction. Ensure people know what you do so they can associate this with you. You'll gain more customers than just keeping quiet about it. In the era of social media and digital marketing, there are so many ways to showcase your business. These tools are most times almost free, don't waste precious time on quiet. Make sure it gets loud.

7.   Legal business.

Know everything about your business. Read up on the laws regulating it. Understand the external rules of the game. Legal structures, accounting system, and business laws are all intricate part of any successful business. It may not be as exciting as the work you do but it is needful and important. Ensure that the business is registered under the right agencies. Learn about your business from anywhere and everywhere.

8. Balance is everything.

Remember that your life is more than just your business. Don't engulf yourself in your work that you forget people around you and the things you love. Your business is a means to an end not the end in itself. As much as you love to work, have time to spend with other people, on yourself, improve your mental, emotional and physical life too. Let your passion drive you to achieve your goals but also be in control of the wheels.

11

BRANDING AND YOUR COMPETITON

Here's the truth, no matter how different you want to be, there are hundreds of businesses out there determined to take that one customer from you. The market place is truly crowded. To be successful, you need to create a brand that beats the competition and stands out from the crowd. Here are some things to look out for when branding your business to beat your competition.

Get innovative. Innovation is never overrated. Come up with new things, explore new territories. Check out other companies in countries away from yours and see what makes them stand out. Don't limit yourself to your own resources. With the internet and apps today, you can be anywhere in the world just by clicking buttons. So get creative with it.

Build a great image. Your business reputation counts a whole lot. Everything that represents your brand must be an expression of what you wish to portray to the market. From choice of colors, shape, size, uniform, to the logo says volume about your business. First impressions can't be changed. Branding is about packaging your business in a way that it stands out from every other one. The perception of your brand will determine how people will react to it. Ensure that what you act out is exactly how you want the business to be. Fake it till you make it.

Deliver your brand promise. Having integrity is great for any business. Making good on your promises will help achieve loyalty from your audience. Figure out what you want to be known for, tell your market what you would give them, and then meet up with it.

Branding is a way to define your business to yourself, your customers and the market place. It is a way of getting noticed and acknowledged in the world where everyone is fighting for attention.

START NOW!

So you've read it all. Don't just wait on your couch.
Go now and get started. Everything big started small.
Start now!

APPRECIATION

We sincerely appreciate your purchase of our book that
reveals useful information about everything you need
to know about Entrepreneurship. We hope you love it!

Thanks!

Sharifah Hardie.